A Definitive Commentary on Bookplates

This edition dedicated to
Fred Stielow,
librarian extraordinary.

A Definitive Commentary on Bookplates

Edward Gordon Craig's
Nothing, or The Bookplate

Edited and introduced by
Paul Rich

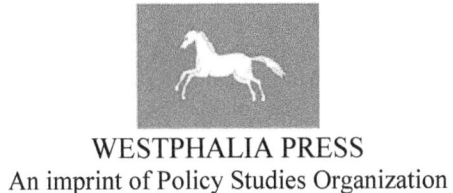

WESTPHALIA PRESS
An imprint of Policy Studies Organization

A Definitive Commentary on Bookplates
Edward Gordon Craig's
Nothing, or The Bookplate

For information:
Westphalia Press
1527 New Hampshire Ave., N.W.
Washington, D.C. 20036

ISBN-13: 978-0-944285-84-8
ISBN-10: 0944285848

Updated material and comments on this edition can be found at the
Policy Studies Organization website: http://www.ipsonet.org/

CRAIG'S BOOKPLATES

*

INTRODUCTION TO THE NEW EDITION

*

EDWARD Gordon Craig was the son of Edward Godwin, who like his son, designed stage sets, and of Ellen Terry, a very famous actress.

Relevant to this book is the fact that he began cutting woodcuts as a boy. The same principle that guided his career as a set designer influenced his work with bookplates. He believed in art as an expression of the imagination.

He was no stranger to publishing. In 1898 he founded a theatre publication called *The Page* and in 1908 *The Mask*. He also produced the short-lived *The Marionette* in 1918. His books included *The Art of the Theatre*, *On the Art of the Stage*, *Towards a New Theatre, Scene, The Theatre Advancing,* and *Books and Theatres,* as well as lives of Henry Irving and his mother.

He was far ahead of his time in his view of stage productions, so it is not surprising that his thoughts on bookplates remain of current interest. His bookplate enthusiasm led him to design more than 200 bookplates, now highly collectible, and to think deeply about their significance. This book by him, despite the passage of years, remains basic to whenever there is discussion about bookplates.

Paul Rich

E

NOTHING OR THE BOOKPLATE

NOTHING

OR

THE BOOKPLATE

BY

EDWARD GORDON CRAIG

WITH A HANDLIST

BY

E. CARRICK

———

El buey sin cencerro pitrdese presto

———

LONDON

J. M. DENT & SONS LTD.

MADE AND PRINTED IN GREAT BRITAIN
AT THE CURWEN PRESS, LONDON
FIRST PUBLISHED IN 1925 BY CHATTO AND WINDUS
RE-ISSUED BY J. M. DENT AND SONS LTD., 1931

FOREWORD

*

WHEN I hear young men telling me that though they love the Theatre more than all else, yet cannot work for it for nothing, cannot give up a comfortable salary in some one theatre and fight for a better theatre, because if they do they will not be able to pay for their rent and food, I think of my bookplates.

For bookplates once served me in good stead. I was a young man, and wanted to fight for a better Theatre, and, to do so, wanted to get away from the old one and study.

To give up my engagement would mean giving up a regular £8 a week. The bookplate in part made it possible for me to do this. Instead of £8 a week, the bookplate brought me about £2 a week. Wood-engraving and drawing for journals helped me too, but bookplates were the chief source of income for me.

So I always remember this, and always feel grateful toward the whole world of bookplates and bookplate collectors, users, and makers.

This is all I shall offer as apology for reprinting the little things—they are old friends.

NOTE

*

THE PUBLISHERS and I wish to thank the ladies and gentlemen who have courteously allowed us to reproduce their bookplates in this book.

And we wish to ask forgiveness from those few—three they are—who, in spite of every attempt to reach them, have somehow eluded us.

I hope that all will be quite right and that they will feel that we have only acted as pirates under compulsion.

If any piracy has taken place, either it has been utterly virtuous or I alone am the culprit. I alone am the captain of this ship and I've been signalling my whereabouts to the said three for many months.

I have signalled 'May I pillage?', but not one semaphore has been seen in reply.

I have signalled 'I intend to pillage,' and all I heard was an echo answering 'Pillage and be blowed!'

Echo has never before invented, she has only echoed, so if only to mark the occasion I decided to pillage and be blowed.

If I may pillage without being blowed—then we are back where we were and Echo returns to her place.

CONTENTS

*

THE BOOKPLATE

FIRST TRIFLES

*

WHAT IT IS, WHAT IT DOES

*

A BOOKPLATE is a trifle: it consists of a small piece of paper,[1] stamped with a name or a device, generally both, or with initials, and pasted on the inside cover of a book to declare the ownership.

A bookplate does this—it serves to protect the book for its owner. A bookplate is to the book what a collar is to the dog, though at present there is no Battersea for books. On the dog's collar one engraves, 'I am Smith's dog.' Alter the word 'dog' to 'book'—add some simple adornment in the shape of a flower, a butterfly, or a crest, and we have what is called a bookplate.

Somehow a large bookplate is an absurdity. The largest bookplate I ever made measured $4\frac{1}{4}$ by $2\frac{1}{4}$ inches, and I consider that too tall by about $2\frac{3}{4}$ inches and too wide by 1 inch. The bookplates for my mother (Figure 4) and my eldest daughter (Figure 10) measured about $4\frac{1}{4}$ by $2\frac{1}{2}$ inches. These I consider were too large, and though I'm sure they'd not say so if you came to ask them, still there are many of their books into which these bookplates will not go, which, after all, is some argument in

[1] Other materials have been and still are used: thin leather is one which, if troublesome to fix in your book by your own hand, is none the less steady, and if the design be good and suited to leather, is worth the expense.

favour of a smaller plate. I made some plates for myself. The largest is $2\frac{1}{2}$ by $1\frac{1}{2}$ inches—the smallest $\frac{3}{4}$ by $\frac{1}{2}$ inch, and I consider that the smallest is the best—I use it most.

And when I say that a plate must be small—a mere nothing— or it is less than nothing, I do not mean that the skill, patience, labour, and taste shown by the engraver of a large bookplate is nothing. His efforts are worthy of the highest praise; but they are often wasted efforts, for to do more when much less is enough is to waste.

A large, imposing, and elaborately worked-up bookplate is annoying—just as a talkative, intellectual, highly cultured footman would be a nuisance. Suppose, on ringing the bell to inquire whether some friend was in, we had the doors thrown open for us by a remarkable man who, with charming gestures bade us enter, bade us be seated, took a seat by us and began to utter a number of very witty or very profound things which held us spellbound and quenched any desire in us to proceed further than the hall. Or suppose he chattered to us to explain how and where his master was, why he was there, what he looked like, what his tastes, where educated, how he was feeling last week, etc.

We wish only one thing from the footman who opens the door. We wish to know, is he in, the master, or is he out, will he see us, or no. And the finely trained footman is the quietest, the least noticeable, one who makes himself small; the perfect footman is a gem.

That is what a bookplate should be—a gem.

It should make itself small. It should be well set, quiet, and should announce whose book it is, and all in as few words and lines as possible. If any people in Europe should be able to do this better than the others it is the English; hence the English bookplates should be the most remarkable, not for their elaboration, but for their repose.

I know of some admirable artists in England who like to make big bookplates. They engrave marvellous things in their own way which are liked; but to me a big, a ponderous bookplate which is a 'masterpiece of the engraver's art' is rather too like a person who is trying to make a fuss. I hate the thing, I wish it ill, for no good bookplate fusses—it makes no scene—it stands back and keeps quiet.

Yet these ponderous plates are sometimes accepted and used by people who have quite distinguished libraries: people who go to the theatre armed with opera-glasses and determined to see what the artist has planned so carefully for them not to see: people who press you two and even three times to eat more when you have already eaten quite enough: people who determine to see all Italy in six days and who do all things so thoroughly that they do not come to see even one little village of Tuscany.

SECOND TRIFLE

*

MY BOOKPLATES

*

I spoke of gems—but I am well aware that my bookplates are not gems. Still, since others have liked them and used them, I bring them together here in the hope of pleasing a few more.

I do not put a great deal of work into a plate, because when I labour very long at anything of this kind I find that I do not improve it, and after a certain time I spoil it. But because this is so in my case, it does not follow that a very much worked-at plate, even if it only measure $2\frac{1}{4}$ centimetres by 2 centimetres, is not, and cannot be, very beautiful. I do not know of many beautiful postage stamps, but an average size postage stamp measures just that, and it contains an amazing amount of work on it. Indeed, I have always held that a postage stamp is, in point of size and adaptability, just what a perfect bookplate should be.

And what should be on it? (Well, certainly not gum, and for a special reason which I will explain later on.) What design besides the name or initials of the owner?

If I were holding a class and speaking to my students, I should say, 'If I were you I should not put anything on your design which cannot reasonably be expected to be found inside the book into which it will be placed.' Saying this, I know I point the finger of scorn at many of my own plates—it cannot be helped.

For example, why, on opening a little miniature volume of eighteenth-century love poems, should I be disagreeably surprised by discovering on the inside cover a dragon and these words in Greek or Latin: ' He who would cross my path, let him beware'? Or why should I find on that quiet first page the portrait of an old monk in a hood or a self-conscious gentleman in silk breeches and a powdered wig, reading — reading another book, a kind of parody of what I myself was intending to do.

I've done it myself: before I got squeamish. I, too, made plates of people reading books, and humanity is so strange and kind that the owners of bookplates of mine prefer my blunders to my virtues. But once or twice I did the correct thing, and may this right rectify the wrong; twice, anyhow once, I made a plate which showed us a violet and its leaf, pressed (Figure 15). On opening the book in which you find that plate, surely it cannot offend—pasted there it refuses to slip—perhaps it should do this and fall on the floor—that is beyond my powers to bring about.

I would call your attention to some other blunders of mine, but you have already seen them, and are as tired of them as I am. So all I would do is to ask you whether you do not agree with me that the most fitting are the plainer, smaller marks. My own small oval G. C. (see cover), for example, and the small I. D. (Figure 19).

THE NUMBER OF BOOKPLATES AND PRINTERS' MARKS DESIGNED AND ENGRAVED BY E. GORDON CRAIG
1895 to 1912

List made by E. Carrick.

1895	2
1896	2
1897	1
1898	21
1899	26
1900	18
1901	21
1902	4
1903	5
1904	1
1905	2
1906	3
1908	8
1910	3
1911	1
1912	4
	122*

*Of these, seven were not engraved, but were reproduced from the designs by a process.

THIRD TRIFLE

*

THE PURCHASER

*

THE worst of it is, that scraps like these do not look worth £25 each, and I understand that is a very moderate price to pay for a really good plate.

Yet it's not how much work, nor how large, nor how elaborate it be which makes it valuable, but how fitting. To hit on the right plate for the right man often means rejecting dozens.

To hit on the very thing is no easy task: it takes time, unless you hit on it by good luck right away. Then to encourage the purchaser to see eye to eye with you until he comes to realize for himself what a good one you've found for him, that's difficult too.

And so it is far easier to make a bookplate for a lady—so gracious about such things—so willing to see as you see. The only fear is that one might become weak and humour all her wishes. But once past these rocks, what easier than to do one's best when it is for a woman one is working? You do not agree? Ah, but I do, when it is a question of a bookplate.

If I have a special fancy, it is for plans of places—plans of houses or towns—with the house of the owner marked clearly. My son has lately made me a new bookplate. It is the plan of an eighteenth-century theatre, measuring one inch and a quarter by three-quarters. I have tried it in my theatre books and I do not find it is in the way.

But here we come to how many different bookplates a man

can use. I should say that if you have a serious library, and love
your books as much as you love your wine, you will do well to
put aside £100 to pay for three or four plates, first letting your
friend the artist go freely ahead, then trying the result in a few
of your books. Unless he hits on the very thing at once, you
will have to be asking him to try again, and then again—
allowing time to pass—coming back to it, being in no hurry
to put a plate in every one of your books until something which
is perfect be evolved—that something-nothing which is the
perfection. If you do this, I think you will not be acting
unwisely.

FOURTH TRIFLE

*

THE PROCESS

*

As for the process which should be employed by the artist, that, I think, may be left to him. For my own part, I prefer a woodcut above every other process: for then the plate will be like the rest of the book, wood block and type being twin brothers—a wood block and type being both printable on the same kind of press and at the same time. I do not like a pen design reproduced by machinery. I do not like the modern process blocks—they can be good when an artist takes them in hand, but as a rule they are no good at all . . . they are not 'sympatico.' And I like a touch of colour, and I like it to be put on by hand.

And this matter concerns the purchaser. I designed my own plate for myself. I am therefore my own purchaser and artist and librarian; and I enjoy enormously putting a small dab of colour on my plates after I have pasted them into a few volumes. I make it yellow for books of a certain order, green for another, or a red, or red and green, or purple, all depending very much on the tone and texture of the end paper on which the plate is pasted. But it also depends a little on my mood—the mood of the purchaser—the owner and lover of the particular volume in hand.

C

LAST TRIFLES

*

You may feel that this is very much too much to be writing about so slight and so insignificant a thing as a bookplate. And so it would be, but for the fact that, as I write, there comes up before me the BOOK itself. No, after all it is not unimportant, for a book is one of the best things we can meet, and book-lovers agree that everything to do with books is a delight.

And if books are so important, should not the bookplates be stamped in gold on the outside of the cover? That, of course, is the real sport; but it is only for those who like, and can afford, their sport to be swagger. I cannot—but I have found a few books stamped so, with some rich owner's mark, and they look superb: such a bookplate becomes part of the architecture of the book. And this being the ideal, it quite rules out all thought of having realistic or pictorial designs on bookplates. We can but deal in marks—a coat-of-arms or initials, and the best book-plates I have ever seen are just that—coats-of-arms, initials, marks.

See the superb mark on the cover of *L'Ipermestra*, which belonged to Cardinal Giovanni Carlo di Toscane, and which is now in the Bibliothèque du Conservatoire Royale du Musique in Brussels; or the *Cabelis Commentarium*, 1551, with the plate of King James the Sixth of Scotland stamped upon it.

But, unfortunately, we are not the Cardinal Giovanni Carlo di Toscane, nor can we ever hope to be James VI. It is just as unlikely that any of us will ever be a prince or a pope, so we must put off our airs and come down to our graces.

Our bookplates must be on paper, and we shall come to enjoy the intense pleasure which awaits us if we will but come down.

The enjoyment is to spend an hour now and then pasting our plate into the book; for paste must be used, never gum. Gum is good and sticky, but gum is also yellow and shows through fine paper, and bookplates look best and are most serviceable when printed on paper which is fine. So use white paste. Another reason against gum is this. Suppose you do get your stationer or your artist to see that the plates are printed on gummed paper. They arrive at your house flat, but in hot weather they will curl up as they lie in the drawer or box, and in damp weather they will stick to one another: so forbid gum to be used.

You paste in a plate as follows. First take down your books— some thirty of them—and put them at your left hand on the empty table. In front of you place your bookplates. These keep out of the sun, lest they curl. In front of you have also a jar of water and a small pot of paste or stick-fast, and a camel-hair paint-brush (Reeves A.8). On no account use the bristled thing which paste-sellers throw in extra and call a brush. Reserve this for your hats or boots, but a good camel-hair brush is better for paste and books. Two more things you must have in front of you, and then you can begin; and these are (1) thirty pieces of blotting-paper (later on you will find fewer will do)—they need not be very large, but must be a little larger than your plate; so take scissors and cut up thirty pieces, and when cut up put in a little pile in front of you with (2) an ivory or wooden paper-knife. Don't put any of these things on the side. When working, all tools and materials should be in front of you. So now your stage is set.

Seated at your table, you have on your left hand your thirty books in, let us say, three piles. Three is the safest, for if in one pile they might topple down. In front of you, ivory paper-knife, paste-pot with paste in it, brush (camel-hair), a jar or pot of water, and thirty to thirty-three bookplates. (Best have a few more than the exact number to prevent your having to get up and search for more later on: should one or two get damaged, be found torn, or in one way or another prove useless.)

On your right hand the deck, or may I say the stage, is cleared.

Take the first book, enjoy looking at it, turn it about, don't discern defects: it's too late now—now enjoyment is your only task. 'Learn to enjoy' is what Nietzsche would say, but I say rather throw the table and its contents out of the window and enjoy a crash if you don't naturally come by enjoyment as you set about this process of sticking your bookplates into your books.

Now put down the book in front of you. It is better to put it the right way up when you do put it down, so as not to discover later that you have pasted the plate on the end cover. Many bookplate pasters do this, that's why I mention the point here.

Having discovered which is the right end of the book, open it and bend back the flap, *i.e.* the cover—be it of boards and paper or boards and leather, or boards and vellum, or cloth—and let this flap or cover rest back on another book:

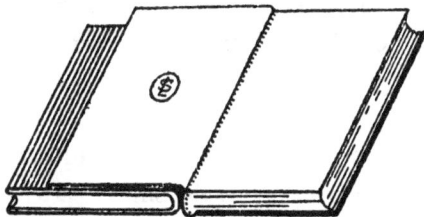

This steadies it. Then take one of your bookplates and thrust it into the jar of water. Turn it around a bit and take it out, and shake off all the water, maybe even lay it face downwards on a sheet of blotting-paper. (I had forgotten to say that an extra large sheet of blotting-paper for working on is always useful, but it is not essential.) While damp, put a dab of paste on the back of the plate as it lies on the paper and spread it around. Don't use too much paste: very little is sufficient. How little? Hardly any. Then pick up the plate by the aid of the paper-knife, this way: thrust the knife under the plate; by this means you will get no paste on your fingers, nor remove paste from the back of the plate. Then judge with your eye the centre of the inner cover of the book to which you desire to affix the plate, and then, 'Let her go, Mr. Asher.'

(I must ask your pardon for this theatricalism, but it will out —like murder. Mr. Asher was a conductor at the Tivoli Music Hall in my youth. Then he was wonderful—now he is a fable. He held thirty to forty master musicians in thrall. At each of his beats the whole thirty or forty musicians sounded one note apiece—or a series of notes. But if he stopped beating, they dared not make a sound. The comic singers would talk, patter they called it, and at the end of a long or short bit of patter they would have immortal longings to pick up their song again and swing along. So to start the thing going, and neatly too, the comedians came to say to Mr. Asher, 'Let her go, Mr. Asher'— 'she' being the combined heart strings and violin strings and trumpets and cymbals and the drums of the thirty or forty master musicians.)

Once the plate is on the cover you may breathe, but it must get into place at once, or not at all: shifting afterwards is not to be thought of. So this part of the trick is something like to swing a pancake. Then take up one of the cut pieces of blotting-paper and place it on the upturned face of the plate. Then press gently. After gentleness use force. Take the paper-knife in the right hand, and holding the blotting-paper very firmly pressed on to the plate with the thumb and finger so as to allow no possible slipping or sliding, press the flat side of the paper-cutter all over the blotting-paper.

Should you have put too much paste on the plate, it will all be squeezed out at the four edges of the plate, and that will spoil things. If you put the fair amount, it will spread evenly, and a little water and a very little paste may appear all around the edges of the plate, but I hope not. But should it appear, it will immediately be sopped up by the blotting-papers.

Then lift the blotting-paper and look upon your work.

It may be that you will find many a fault. The design may not be quite straightly placed, or, though straight, may not be exactly in the middle of the cover. For my part, I like to see a plate sometimes placed anywhere but exactly in the middle. Still, as a rule, let it be at equal distances from each side, but rather farther from the lower edge and rather nearer the upper edge. If it appear to be more out of the desired position than you expected, and askew, it is quite possible that it has shifted as you pressed on the blotting-paper. Unless you hold the blotting-paper very steadily with the left hand, the bookplate will shift as you press and rub with the paper-knife.

The plate once fixed, do not close the book unless you must. Better leave it open to dry, placing it on the clear space of table to your right. If you must close it up, be careful to put a piece of blotting-paper just over it, or it will damp the sheet of white or coloured paper which we call an end paper, and the damp will in time damage the book.

(By the way, when an end paper is brown or blue or many coloured, be careful before you decide which of your bookplates shall go on it. Too often a bookplate is ruined by colour coming off the sheet facing it.)

One book having been successfully labelled, label the rest. Thirty may be enough to do at a sitting. If you will take my advice you will let no one else do the work.

This is my idea of being practical about bookplates. I can imagine them, design them, cut them, sell them now and again, use them when I have time, enjoy them always.

I won't say anything more except to remind you that my real vocation is the Theatre, and not the making of bookplates. In bookplate making I bow before the masters who stride before me in all their glory. It has been a great pleasure to collect these scraps together, for I have been thinking that perhaps some young theatre fellow will be encouraged to emulate me in this, my second calling, of label maker—because it will enable him to make £2 a week—stop doing bad stage work for a large weekly salary and turn to the study of the stage, and someday, perhaps, bless me.

LIST OF BOOKPLATES & SOME PRINTERS' MARKS

DESIGNED & ENGRAVED ON WOOD OR METAL

BY E. GORDON CRAIG

1895 TO 1912

*

¶ 1895
1. NO OWNER:
Female figure, side view, with garland. *Not signed. Size* $2\frac{5}{8}$ × 2 *ins.*

2. E. GORDON CRAIG:
A flower with the initials 'G. C.' *Not signed. Size* $1\frac{3}{32}$ × $\frac{7}{8}$ *inches.*

¶ 1896
3. GORDON CRAIG:
A flower, with the initials 'G. C. 1896' in borderlines. *Not signed. Size* $2\frac{5}{8}$ × $1\frac{17}{32}$ *inches.*

4. S. B. BRERTON:
Female before a stand with book, with the initials 'S. B. B. his book.' *Signed G. C. '96, in borderlines. Size* $2\frac{5}{8}$ × $1\frac{19}{32}$ *inches.*

¶ 1897
5. LUCY WILSON:
Female figure with sword, with the initials 'L. W. '97' in borderlines. *Not signed. Size* $2\frac{5}{8}$ × $1\frac{7}{16}$ *inches.*

¶ 1898
6. GORDON CRAIG:
A flower, with the initials 'G. C 1898' in borderlines. *Not signed. Size* $2\frac{9}{16}$ × $1\frac{1}{2}$ *inches.*

7. NO OWNER:
Female figure, side view, in borderlines. *Not signed. Size* $2\frac{7}{16}$ × $1\frac{19}{32}$ *ins.*

8. ELLEN TERRY:
Plan of Winchelsea, with the words 'Winchelsea Ex Libris Ellen Terry.' *In double borderlines. Signed G. C. '98. Size* $4\frac{1}{4}$ × $2\frac{3}{4}$ *ins.*

D

9. EDITH CRAIG:

A rose in a circle, with the word 'Edy.' *Not signed. Size* 1 $\frac{5}{32}$ *inches diameter.*

10. ROSIE CRAIG

Rose with long stem with initials '1898 Ex Libris R. C.' *Signed P. Size* 4 $\frac{8}{16}$ × 1 $\frac{1}{16}$ *inches.* (Figure 10.)

11. M.M.

A Pierrot with flag. Initials 'Ex libris MM.' *Not signed. Borderlines. Size* 3 $\frac{7}{8}$ × 1 $\frac{1}{16}$ *inches.*

12. MARTIN SHAW:

A musician tuning a lute, with initials 'M. S.' *Signed C in borderlines. Size* 1 $\frac{1}{4}$ × $\frac{23}{32}$ *inches.*

13. EDITH CRAIG:

Girl holding a book, with words 'Edy her book.' *Signed C. in borderlines. Size* 2 $\frac{11}{16}$ × 1 $\frac{7}{16}$ *inches.*

14. T. NORMAN

Figure of girl with book and initials 'Ex Libris T. N.' *Two borderlines. Not signed. Size* 1 $\frac{1}{4}$ × 1 $\frac{1}{16}$ *inches.*

15. GEOFFREY SHAW:

Map of British Isles, with initials 'Ex libris G. T. S.' in borderlines. *Not signed. Size* 2 $\frac{5}{16}$ × 2 $\frac{7}{32}$ *inches.*

16. EDIE LANE:

A guinea-pig, with initials E. D. L. *Not signed. Size* $\frac{3}{4}$ × 1 $\frac{5}{32}$ *inches.*

17. GORDON CRAIG:

Flower in circle (white on black) with initials 'G. C.' *Not Signed. Size* $\frac{7}{8}$ *inch diameter.*

18. GORDON CRAIG

Small flower with initials 'G. C.' *Not signed. Size* $\frac{15}{32}$ × $\frac{1}{2}$ *inches.*

19. KATIE BLACK:

Hill with town and sun, with 'Ex Libris Katie Black.' *In borderlines. Signed C. Size* 3 $\frac{17}{32}$ × 2 $\frac{3}{4}$ *inches.*

20. G. PHILLIPSON & SON, Printers:

A rose and leaves with initials 'A. P. and 'E. B. P.' in top corners. In centre 'G. P. Printers: Kingston-on-Thames, Surrey, 1898.' *In borderlines. Signed C. Size* 1 $\frac{23}{32}$ × 1 $\frac{7}{16}$ *inches.*

21. JAMES PRYDE:

A sailing ship, with 'Ex Libris James Pryde 1898.' *Not signed. Size* 2 $\frac{3}{16}$ × 1 $\frac{11}{16}$ *inches.* (Figure 11.)

22. J. D.

Plan of a theatre with initials 'J. D.' *Borderlines. Not signed. Size* $3\frac{3}{32}$ × $2\frac{5}{32}$ *inches.*

23. NO OWNER:

Female figure reclining. *In borderlines. Not signed. Size* $2\frac{11}{16}$ × $1\frac{9}{16}$ *inches.*

24. NO OWNER:

Man reading. *In borderlines. Not signed. Size* $1\frac{23}{32}$ × $1\frac{1}{4}$ *inches.*

25. NO OWNER:

Two cornucopias encircling a female figure. *Signed C. Size c.* $3\frac{3}{4}$ *inches diameter.*

26. NO OWNER:

Lake, houses, and rainbow. Square. *In borderlines. Not signed. Size* $2\frac{1}{16}$ × $2\frac{1}{16}$ *inches.*

❡ 1899

27. GORDON CRAIG:

Small acorn with initials 'G. C.' *Not signed. Size* $\frac{23}{32}$ × $\frac{7}{8}$ *inches.*

28. ELLEN TERRY:

A bouquet, with initials 'E. T. 1899.' *In borderlines. Signed E. Size* $1\frac{7}{64}$ × $\frac{27}{32}$ *inches.*

29. ELLEN TERRY:

A bouquet with initials 'E. T. 1899.' *Signed G. C. Size* $1\frac{6}{16}$ × $1\frac{1}{4}$ *inches.* (Figure 5.)

30. ROBIN CRAIG:

Toy cock with initials 'R. C. 1899.' On black background. *Not signed. Size* $1\frac{9}{16}$ × $1\frac{8}{32}$ *inches.*

31. CISSY LOFTUS:

Wreath and ribbons with initials 'C. L. 1899.' *Borderlines. Signed C. Size* $1\frac{3}{16}$ × $\frac{13}{16}$ *inches.*

32. OLIVER BATH:

Branch of a herb with: 'Oliver Bath 1899.' *Signed G. C. Borderlines. Size* $2\frac{8}{32}$ × $1\frac{23}{32}$ *inches.* (Figure 18.)

33. AUDREY CAMPBELL:

Small wreath with initials 'A. C.' *Not signed. Size* $\frac{23}{32}$ *inches diameter.*

34. GABRIELLE ENTHOVEN:

Basket of flowers with initials 'G. E.' *Not signed. Size* $1\frac{8}{32}$ × $2\frac{3}{16}$ *inches.* (Figure 17.)

35. HELEN FOX:

A toy jack-in-a-box with initials 'H. F.' *In borderlines. Signed C. Size* $1\frac{3}{32}$ × $1\frac{3}{32}$ *inches.* (Figure 23.)

36. ELLEN TERRY:

Plan of Winchelsea (same as No. 8, but recut). *Signed G. C. '99. In double borderlines. Size* 4$\frac{3}{16}$ × 2$\frac{5}{8}$ *inches*. (Figure 4.) *Another state exists reduced to* 1$\frac{17}{32}$ × $\frac{31}{32}$ *inches*. (Figure 4A.)

37. EDITH CRAIG:

A bonnet with initials 'E. C.' *Not signed. Size* 2$\frac{1}{4}$ × 1$\frac{1}{8}$ *inches*. (Figure 1.)

38. CARL MICHAELIS:

Toy poodle with initials 'Ex Libris C. M. 1899'. *In borderlines. Signed G. C. Size* 2$\frac{19}{32}$ × 2$\frac{9}{32}$ *inches*.

39. MARGARET TOLLE-MACHE:

A daisy and other flowers surrounded by a motto. Initials 'Ex Libris M. T. 1899.' *Signed C. Size* 2$\frac{31}{32}$ × 2$\frac{7}{32}$ *inches*. (Figure 8.)

40. CHRISTOPHER ST. JOHN:

Daisy with initial 'C.' *Signed C. Size* 1$\frac{13}{16}$ × 1$\frac{13}{32}$ *inches*.

41. PHILIP CRAIG:

Toy soldier on horse. *Not signed. Initials 'P. C.' In borderlines. Size* 2 × 2 *inches*.

42. GEOFFREY TOLLE-MACHE:

A tortoise with initials 'Ex libris G. T.' *Borderlines.* Below borderlines the motto ' Cercato no sempre solitaria vita.' *Signed G. C. Size* 1$\frac{29}{32}$ × 1$\frac{23}{32}$ *inches*.

43. JOHN DREW:

The Globe Theatre, fence and two figures, with initials 'J. D.' *Signed C. Size* 1$\frac{19}{16}$ × 1$\frac{17}{32}$ *inches*. (Figure 16.)

44. MARGARET PAL-GRAVE:

Bouquet tied with ribbons, with initials 'M. P.' *Signed C. Size* 1$\frac{5}{8}$ × 1$\frac{6}{32}$ *inches*.

45. ELLEN TERRY:

Small wreath with initials 'E. A. T.' in centre. *Borderlines. Not signed. Size* $\frac{9}{16}$ × $\frac{17}{32}$ *inches*.

46. GORDON CRAIG:

Flower on small oval shield, with initials 'G. C.' *Not signed. Size* $\frac{23}{32}$ × $\frac{5}{8}$ *inches*. (Cover.)

47. AIMÉE LOWTHER:

Flowers, torch, arrows, quiver and mask, tied with ribbons on which are the very small initials 'E. A. T.' with large initials 'A. L.' *Signed C. Size* 2$\frac{3}{32}$ × 2$\frac{7}{16}$ *inches*. (Figure 6.)

48. MARION TERRY:

A wreath with initials 'M. T. 1899.' *Borderlines. Signed G. C. Size* $3\frac{11}{16}$ $\times$ $2\frac{7}{16}$ *inches.*

49. NO OWNER:

A bell with date 1899, signed c. *Size* $\frac{7}{8} \times 1\frac{1}{4}$ *inches.*

50. FARNCOMBE & Son Printer:

Flowers, with initials 'F. F. Printer Croydon 1890.' *Signed C. Size* $1\frac{7}{8}$ $\times$ $1\frac{1}{4}$ *inches.*

51. NO OWNER:

Two rosebuds. *Not signed. Size* $1\frac{3}{32} \times 1\frac{13}{16}$ *inches.*

52. M. M.

A flower with initials 'M. M.' White on black. *Size* $1\frac{1}{16} \times \frac{1}{2}$ *inches.*

¶ 1900
53. E. F. HOWARD:

A ship and waves with initials E. F. H.' *Signed G. C. 1900. Size* $1\frac{1}{16} \times \frac{31}{32}$ *inches.*

54. ELLEN TERRY:

Small flower with initials 'E. T.' White on black. *Not signed. Size* $\frac{9}{16} \times \frac{1}{2}$ *inches.*

55. J. D.

Small flower with initials 'J. D.' *Not signed. Size* $\frac{1}{2} \times \frac{3}{8}$ inches.

56. PAMELA COLEMAN SMITH:

Pressed violets and leaves. Initials 'P. S.' *Signed C. Size* $3 \times 1\frac{21}{32}$ *inches.* (Figure 15.)

57. ELLEN TERRY:

A bunch of grapes with 'E. T.' *Signed C. Size* $\frac{7}{8} \times 1\frac{5}{32}$ *inches.*

58. LINDSAY JARDINE:

Two flowers in a pot with 'Lindsay 1900.' *Not signed. Size* $1\frac{1}{4} \times 1\frac{5}{16}$ *inches.* (Figure 7.)

59. CHARLES DALMON:

Branch of a herb with initials 'C. D.' *Signed C. Size* $2\frac{1}{2} \times 1\frac{3}{4}$ *inches.*

60. HALDANE MACFALL:

Figure reading by a lake with 'Haldane Macfall his book.' *In borderlines. Signed G. C.* 1 (*i.e.* 1901). *Size* $3\frac{7}{8} \times 3\frac{1}{4}$ *inches.* (Figure 14.)

61. W. H. DOWNING:

A ship with the words 'Ex Libris W. H. Downing.' *Borderlines. Signed Craig. (Not Engraved.) Size* $2\frac{7}{8} \times 2\frac{3}{8}$ *inches.*

62. WILLIAM WINTER:

Cottage with garden (Dunmow), with 'This book belongs to William Winter G. C.' *Block signed C. Size* $1\frac{11}{32} \times 2\frac{3}{8}$ *inches.* (Figure 12.)

63. CARLO ROCHE:

Castle on rock with sun behind and name 'Roche 1900.' *Signed G. C. Size* $1\frac{1}{4} \times 1$ *inches.*

64. GORDON CRAIG:

Large acorn with initials 'G. C.' *Not signed. Size* $1\frac{3}{16} \times \frac{7}{8}$ *inches.*

65. BEATRICE TOLLE-MACHE:

A poodle with 'Ex Libris B. T. 1900.' *Signed G. C. Size* $2\frac{31}{32} \times 2\frac{7}{32}$ *inches.*

66. FARNCOMBE & SON, Printer:

Flower with initials 'F. F. Printer Croydon 1900.' *Signed C. Size* $2\frac{19}{32} \times 1\frac{11}{16}$ *inches.*

67. NO OWNER:

Female figure with bouquet. In borderlines. Space for name of owner. *Signed C. Size* $1\frac{3}{4} \times \frac{3}{4}$ *inches.*

68. NO OWNER:

A single rose. *Not signed. Size* $2\frac{1}{8} \times \frac{3}{4}$ *inches.*

69. JUTTA BELL RANSKI:

A crown with ribbons and initials 'J. B. R.' *Borderlines. Not signed. Size* $4\frac{21}{32} \times 2\frac{9}{16}$ *inches.* (Figure 2.)

70. KITTY DOWNING:

A cat on a mat, with initials 'K. D. 1900.' *Signed C. In borderlines. Size* $2\frac{1}{4} \times 1\frac{25}{32}$ *inches.*

¶ 1901

71. LADY RIDLEY:

Rose bush in box, with initials 'A. R.' *Signed C. Size* $3\frac{1}{8} \times 1\frac{1}{2}$ *inches.*

72. N. F. DRYHURST:

Town on hill with initials 'N. F. D.' *In borderlines. Signed C. Size* $1\frac{13}{16} \times 1\frac{11}{32}$ *inches.*

73. BEATRICE IRWIN:

Snake in glass box with initial 'B.' (another state exists of this block, i.e. without the box.) *Not signed. Size* $2 \times 1\frac{31}{32}$ *inches.* (Figure 9, second state.)

74. GORDON CRAIG:

Tree enclosed in borderlines, with initials 'G. C. 1901.' *Not signed. Size* $1\frac{5}{8} \times 1$ *inches.* (Figure 25.)

75. CORA BROWN POTTER:

A fan, a rose, with 'Ex Libris C. B. P.' *Signed C. Size* $2\frac{9}{16} \times 1\frac{11}{16}$ *inches.* (Figure 13.)

76. NO OWNER:

Side view of a mask in borderlines. *Signed C. Size* $1\frac{9}{32} \times 1$ *inches.*

77. LADY CORBET:

A Pink, with the name 'NINA.' *Signed C. Size* $2\frac{3}{16} \times \frac{31}{32}$ *inches.* (Figure 3.)

78. C. MARGARET WATSON:

An Orange-tree in a box, with initials 'C. M. W.' *Not signed.* (*Not engraved.*) *Size* $1\frac{1}{4} \times \frac{15}{16}$ *inches.*

79. JAMES CORBET:

A chicken with 'Ex Libris James Corbet.' *Signed G. C. Size* $1 \times 1\frac{3}{32}$ *inches.*

80. VINCENT CORBET:

A rabbit with initials 'V. C.' *Signed C. Size* $1\frac{1}{2} \times 2\frac{3}{4}$ *inches.*

81. LOUIS BUDDY the third:

A strawberry with initials 'L. B. 3.' *Signed C. Borderlines. Size* $2\frac{11}{16} \times 2\frac{1}{8}$ *inches.*

82. JUTTA BELL RANSKI:

A white rose with initials J. B. R. *Borderlines. Signed G. C. Size* $3\frac{1}{8} \times 1\frac{1}{2}$ *inches.*

83. W. H. B.

A pot of flowers and butterfly with initials 'W. H. B.' *Signed* '*G. C.* 1901' *in type. Size* $1\frac{27}{32} \times 1\frac{5}{16}$ *inches.*

84. PAMELA COLEMAN SMITH:

Miniature stage with figure, and name 'Pamela' in type. *Not signed. Size* $\frac{3}{4} \times \frac{3}{4}$ *inch.*

85. ELENA GORDON CRAIG:

A tree with the word 'Nell 1901.' *Size* $2\frac{13}{16} \times 2\frac{1}{32}$ *inches.*

86. J. W. B.

A bird, with initials 'J. W. B.' *In borderlines. Size* $\frac{29}{32} \times 1\frac{1}{16}$ *inches.*

87. D'ARTAGNAN:

A flower, with initials 'd'A.' White on black background. *In borderlines. Size* $1\frac{1}{4} \times \frac{15}{16}$ *inches.*

88. G. B.

A wreath encircling the initials 'G. B.' *Signed C. Size* 1 $\frac{13}{16}$ *inches diameter.*

89. NO OWNER:

White flower on grey background. *Size* 2 $\frac{9}{32}$ × $\frac{29}{32}$ *inches.*

90. NO OWNER:

Half-length figure of lady in cape. *In borderlines. Signed C. Size* 1 $\frac{13}{16}$ × 1 $\frac{1}{2}$ *inches.*

91. K. F. M. S.

A rose tree with initials 'K. F. M. S. 1901.' *Signed G. C. In double borderlines. Size* 1 $\frac{9}{16}$ × $\frac{29}{32}$ *inches.*

¶ **1902**

92. H. W. NEVINSON:

Mercury's hat with initials 'H. W. N.' *Signed C. Size* 2 $\frac{15}{32}$ × 1 $\frac{7}{8}$ *inches.*

93. NO OWNER:

A tree with a view of Rye, made for Mr Henry James, but not sent. *Size* 1 $\frac{13}{16}$ × 2 $\frac{7}{8}$ *inches.* (Figure 21.)

94. BRIDGES:

Castle on hill with 'Bridges his book.' *Borderlines. Signed G. C. Size* 1 $\frac{17}{32}$ × 1 $\frac{5}{32}$ *inches.*

95. NO OWNER:

Two flowers with their stems entwined. *Size* 1 $\frac{5}{8}$ × 1 $\frac{3}{8}$ *inches.*

¶ **1903**

96. EVELYN SMALLEY:

Landscape with name 'Evelyn Smalley.' *In borderlines. Signed C. (Not engraved.) Size* 1 $\frac{1}{2}$ × 2 $\frac{13}{16}$ *inches.*

97. MARY BOND FOOTE:

The name surrounded by a borderline of flowers. *Not signed. (Not engraved.) Size* $\frac{3}{4}$ × 2 $\frac{7}{16}$ *inches.*

98. SIDNEY PAINTER:

Ship firing gun with initial 'S.' *In borderlines. Signed C. Size* 2 $\frac{7}{16}$ × 2 $\frac{5}{32}$ *inches.*

99. SIDNEY PAINTER:

Tree in circle with 'Sidney Painter.' *In borderlines. Signed G. C. Size* 2 $\frac{21}{32}$ × 2 $\frac{5}{32}$ *inches.*

100. M. M.

A rose with initials 'M. M.' *Signed C. (Not engraved.) Size* $\frac{3}{4}$ × $\frac{15}{16}$ *ins.*

¶ **1904**

101. LINA MILLMAN:

Tower of London with 'One of Lina Millman's books.' *In borderlines. Signed G. C. 1904. Reproduced by half-tone process. Size* 3 $\frac{5}{16}$ × 4 $\frac{11}{16}$ *inches.*

¶ 1905

102. ISADORA DUNCAN:
Flowers growing, with initials 'I. D. 1905.' *Not Signed. Size* $1\frac{1}{64} \times \frac{13}{16}$ *inches.* (Figure 19.)

103. A. and S.
Flowers and butterflies with initials 'A. & S.' *Not signed. Size* $\frac{23}{32} \times \frac{7}{8}$ *inches.*

¶ 1906

104. JAN C. de VOS:
Roman soldier, with 'Ex Libris Jan C. de Vos.' *Not signed. In borderlines. Size* $2\frac{5}{8} \times 1\frac{23}{32}$ *inches.*

105. ROTTERDAM KUNST KRING:
Initials 'R. K. K.' *Not signed. Size* $\frac{23}{32} \times 1\frac{23}{32}$ *inches.*

106. EDMUND MEYER:
Bookseller's mark. Tree with initials 'E. M.' *Size* $1\frac{3}{8} \times \frac{5}{8}$ *inches.*

¶ 1908

107. JULIUS ROLSHO-VEN:
Small circular design of Torre dei Diavoli, Firenze. *Not signed. Size* $1\frac{1}{4}$ *inches diameter.*

E

108. R. P.
A chimera with initials 'R. P.' *Signed C. (Only 5 copies exist with initials; they were cut away later.) Size* $2\frac{7}{16}$ *inches diameter.*

109. M. B.
Flower with initials 'M. B.' (cut in 1898). *Size* $\frac{13}{16} \times \frac{9}{16}$ *inches.*

110. RAY:
A rose with the name 'Ray.' *Not signed. Size* $1\frac{5}{16} \times \frac{5}{8}$ *inches.*

111. NO OWNER:
Circular design with figure in centre. Borderline. *Not signed. Size* $1\frac{1}{4}$ *inches diameter.* (Figure 24.)

112. KARIN:
A bouquet with the name 'Karin. *Not signed. Size* $1\frac{1}{8} \times \frac{3}{4}$ *inches.*

113. KARIN:
A bouquet with the name 'Karin. *Signed C. In borderlines. Size* $1\frac{15}{32} \times 1\frac{1}{4}$ *inches.*

114. WOOD-ENGRAVERS of S. LEONARDO:
Figures under some trees. *Size* $1\frac{1}{16} \times \frac{7}{8}$ *inches.*

¶ 1910

115. NO OWNER:
The letter D. and a small figure riding a skeleton. *In borderlines. Not signed. Size* 1 $\frac{11}{16}$ × 1 $\frac{11}{16}$ *inches.*

116. DOROTHY N. LEES:
The letter D. and architecture in the background. *In borderlines. Not signed. Size* $\frac{5}{8}$ × $\frac{9}{16}$ *inches.*

117. NO OWNER:
The letter 'O' with trees and birds. *In borderlines. Signed C. Size* 2 $\frac{5}{16}$ × 2 $\frac{7}{16}$ *inches.* (Figure 22.)

¶ 1911

118. B. da COSTA GREEN:
A bouquet with the initials: 'B; daC. G.' *Signed G. C.* 1911. *(Etched.) Size* 1 $\frac{7}{8}$ × 1 $\frac{1}{4}$ *inches.*

¶ 1912

119. G. W. PLANK:
Tower with initial 'P.' *Not signed. Size* 2 $\frac{1}{8}$ × 1 $\frac{11}{32}$ *inches.* (Figure 20.)

120. PORTIA KNIGHT:
Pyramid with initials 'P. K.' *Not signed. In borderlines. Size* $\frac{13}{16}$ × $\frac{3}{4}$ *inches.*

121. W. F. GABLE:
Bookworm and sun with initials 'W. G.' *In borderlines. Signed C. Size* 2 $\frac{5}{8}$ *inches diameter.*

122. W. F. GABLE:
Tower with creeper. *Signed C. In borderlines. Size* 2 $\frac{3}{16}$ × 1 $\frac{11}{32}$ *inches.*

ORDER OF THE BOOKPLATES

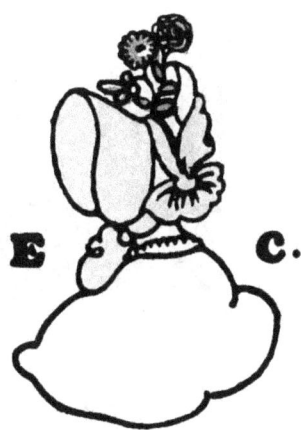

Fig. 1. EDITH CRAIG (37)*
* Numbers in brackets refer to the Chronological List.

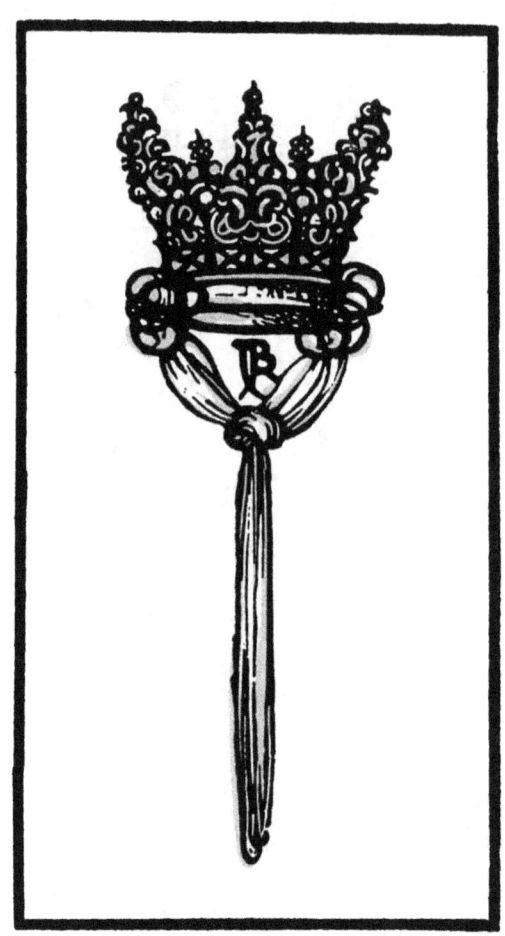

Fig. 2. JUTTA BELL RANSKI (69)

F

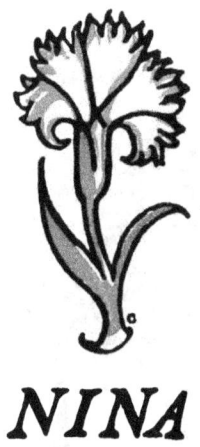

NINA

Fig. 3. LADY CORBET (77)

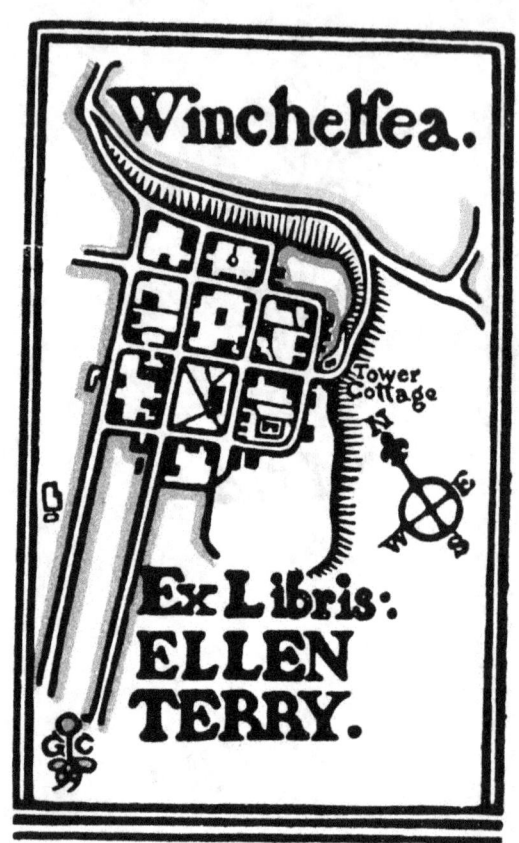

Fig. 4. ELLEN TERRY (36)

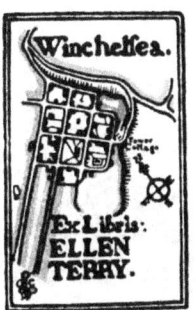

Fig. 4A. ELLEN TERRY (36)

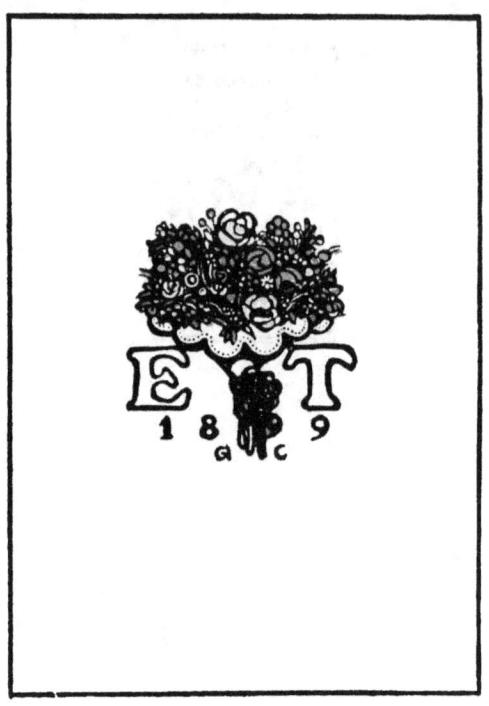

Fig 5. ELLEN TERRY (29)

G

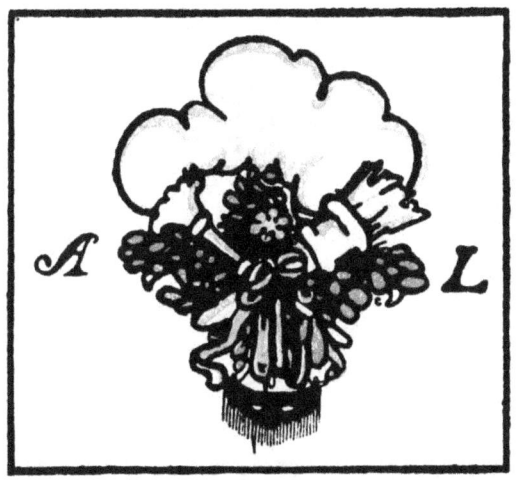

Fig. 6. AIMÉE LOWTHER (47)

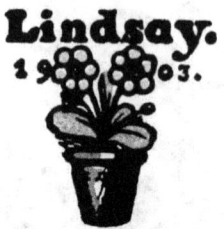

Fig. 7. LINDSAY JARDINE (58)

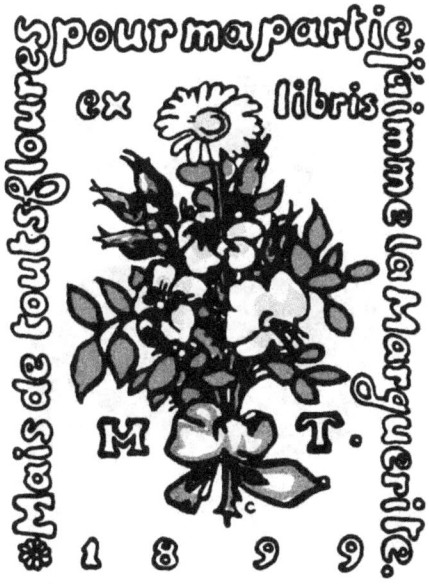

Fig. 8. Margaret Tollemache (39)

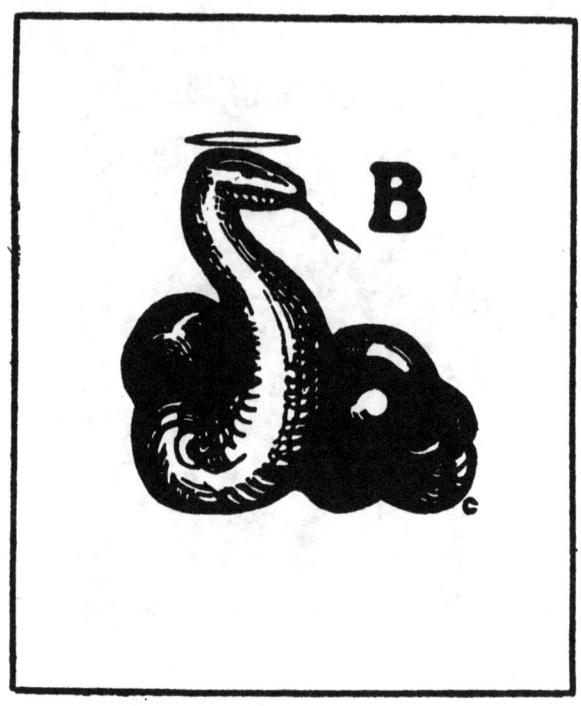

Fig. 9. BEATRICE IRWIN (73)

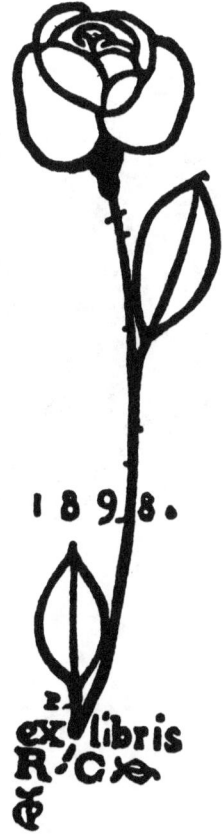

Fig. 10. ROSIE CRAIG (10)

Fig. 11. James Pryde (21)

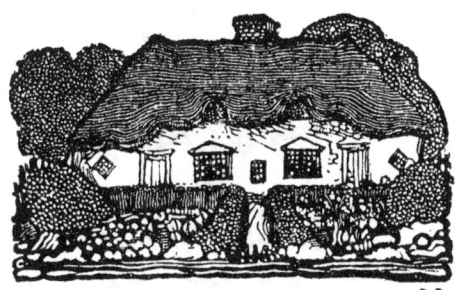

Fig. 12. WILLIAM WINTER (62)

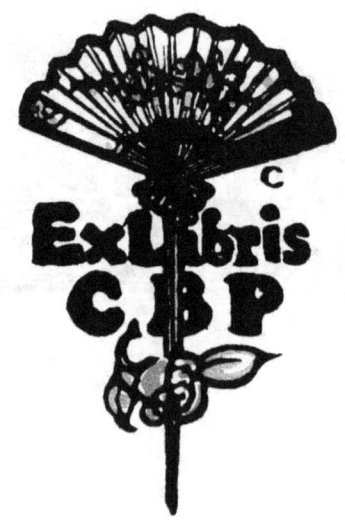

Fig. 13. CORA BROWN POTTER (75)

I

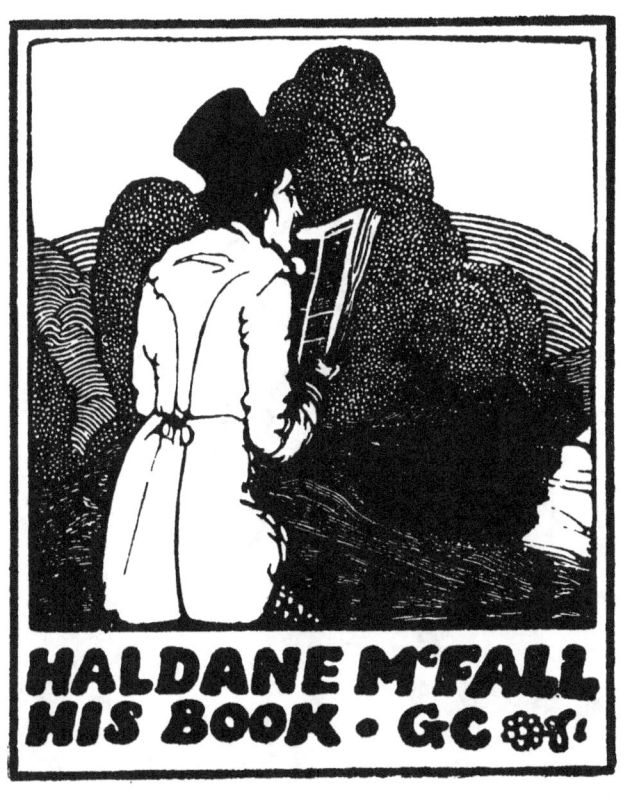

Fig. 14. HALDANE MACFALL (60)

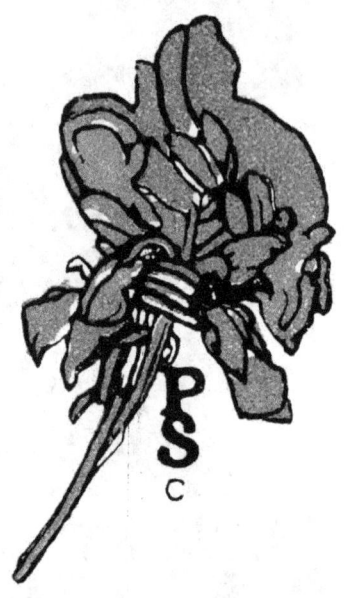

Fig. 15. Pamela Coleman Smith (56)

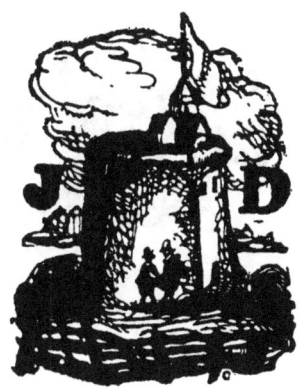

Fig. 16. John Drew (43)

Fig. 17. Gabrielle Enthoven (34)

K

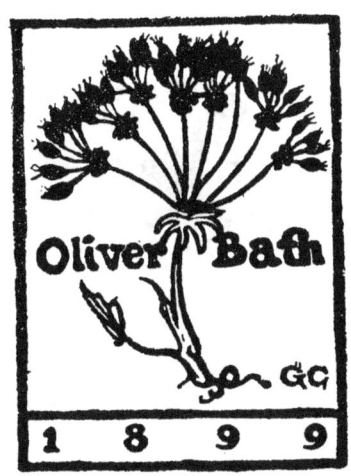

Fig. 18. OLIVER BATH (32)

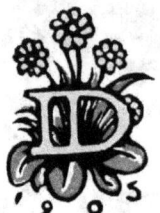

Fig. 19. ISADORA DUNCAN (102)

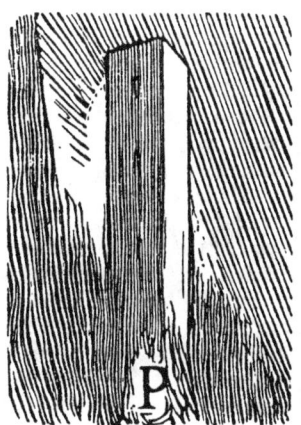

Fig. 20. G. W. PLANK (119)

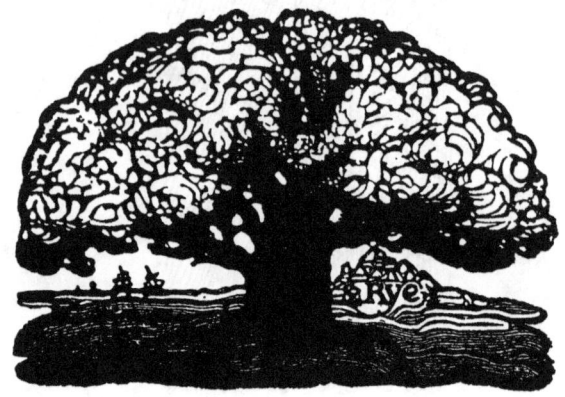

Fig. 21. No Owner (93)

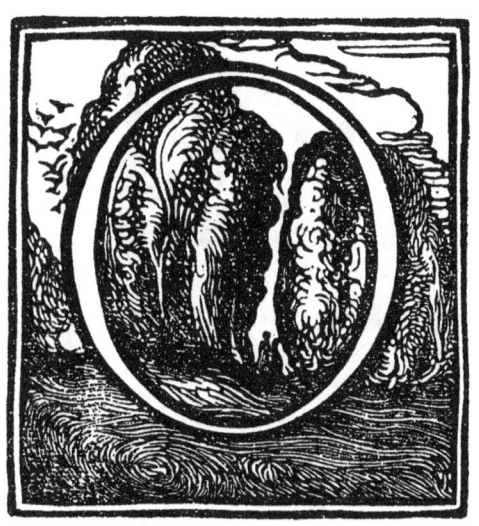

Fig. 22. No Owner (117)

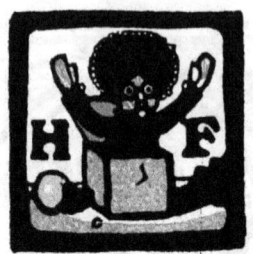

Fig. 23. HELEN FOX (35)

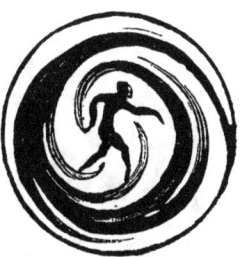

Fig. 24. No Owner (111)

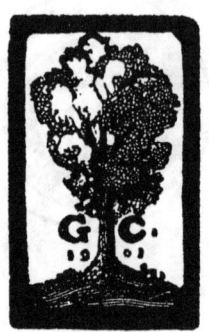

Fig. 25 GORDON CRAIG (74)

www.ingramcontent.com/pod-product-compliance
Lightning Source LLC
Chambersburg PA
CBHW080824170526
45158CB00009B/2513